# 50 French Bread Recipes for Home

By: Kelly Johnson

# Table of Contents

- Baguette Tradition
- Pain de Campagne
- Pain de Mie
- Pain Complet
- Pain Poilâne
- Pain Viennois
- Pain de Seigle
- Pain de Noix
- Pain de Céréales
- Pain d'Épices Baguette
- Pain aux Noix et Raisins
- Pain aux Olives
- Pain de Provence
- Pain de Petit Épeautre
- Pain de Sarrasin
- Pain aux Fruits Secs
- Pain de Courgettes
- Pain au Levain Naturel
- Pain à l'Ancienne
- Pain de Maïs
- Pain de Lentilles
- Pain de Quinoa
- Pain de Tomates Séchées
- Pain aux Herbes de Provence
- Pain aux Figues
- Pain à l'Ail
- Pain de Champagne
- Pain au Fromage
- Pain à la Bière
- Pain à la Châtaigne
- Pain de Pesto
- Pain aux Épinards
- Pain aux Champignon
- Pain de Noël
- Pain à la Citrouille

- Pain de Poires et Roquefort
- Pain de Pommes et Cannelle
- Pain de Pistache
- Pain de Saumon
- Pain de Jambon et Fromage
- Pain à la Banane
- Pain de Citron
- Pain aux Cerises
- Pain de Chocolat
- Pain de Mûres
- Pain à la Lavande
- Pain de Figue et Chèvre
- Pain de Roquefort et Noix
- Pain de Feta et Épinards
- Pain à l'Oignon et au Thym

**Baguette Tradition**

Ingredients:

- 500g all-purpose flour
- 350ml lukewarm water
- 10g salt
- 7g active dry yeast

Instructions:

In a small bowl, mix the active dry yeast with lukewarm water. Let it sit for 5-10 minutes until frothy.
In a large mixing bowl, combine the flour and salt. Create a well in the center.
Pour the activated yeast mixture into the well.
Gradually incorporate the flour into the liquid, stirring with a wooden spoon or your hands until a dough forms.
Knead the dough on a floured surface for about 10 minutes until it becomes smooth and elastic.
Place the dough in a lightly oiled bowl, cover with a damp cloth, and let it rise in a warm place for 1-2 hours or until it doubles in size.
Preheat your oven to 220°C (425°F).
Punch down the risen dough and turn it onto a floured surface. Divide it into two equal portions.
Roll each portion into a long, thin log, shaping it into the classic baguette form.
Place the shaped baguettes on a lightly floured or parchment-lined baking sheet.
Score the tops of the baguettes with a sharp knife or razor blade.
Allow the baguettes to rest for 15-20 minutes.
Bake in the preheated oven for 20-25 minutes or until the crust is golden brown and the bread sounds hollow when tapped.
Cool on a wire rack before slicing.

Enjoy your delicious homemade Baguette Tradition!

## Pain de Campagne

Ingredients:

- 500g bread flour
- 100g whole wheat flour
- 350ml lukewarm water
- 10g salt
- 7g active dry yeast
- 1 tablespoon honey

Instructions:

In a small bowl, combine the active dry yeast, lukewarm water, and honey. Allow it to sit for 5-10 minutes until the mixture becomes frothy.

In a large mixing bowl, combine the bread flour and whole wheat flour. Make a well in the center.

Pour the yeast mixture into the well and gradually incorporate the flour into the liquid, mixing with a wooden spoon or your hands until a dough forms.

Knead the dough on a floured surface for about 10-15 minutes until it is smooth and elastic.

Place the dough in a lightly oiled bowl, cover it with a damp cloth, and let it rise in a warm place for 1-2 hours or until it has doubled in size.

Preheat your oven to 220°C (425°F).

Punch down the risen dough and turn it onto a floured surface. Shape it into a round or oval loaf.

Place the shaped dough on a parchment-lined or floured baking sheet.

Score the top of the bread with a sharp knife or razor blade.

Allow the bread to rest for an additional 15-20 minutes.

Bake in the preheated oven for 30-35 minutes or until the crust is golden brown, and the bread sounds hollow when tapped.

Cool the Pain de Campagne on a wire rack before slicing.

This rustic country bread is perfect for serving with soups, salads, or as a side to your favorite dishes. Enjoy your homemade Pain de Campagne!

**Pain de Mie**

Ingredients:

- 500g all-purpose flour
- 300ml lukewarm milk
- 50g unsalted butter, softened
- 10g sugar
- 10g salt
- 7g active dry yeast

Instructions:

In a small bowl, combine the lukewarm milk and sugar. Stir until the sugar is dissolved. Sprinkle the active dry yeast over the mixture, give it a gentle stir, and let it sit for 5-10 minutes until frothy.
In a large mixing bowl, combine the flour and salt. Create a well in the center.
Add the softened butter and activated yeast mixture into the well.
Gradually incorporate the flour into the liquid, mixing with a wooden spoon or your hands until a dough forms.
Knead the dough on a floured surface for about 10-15 minutes until it becomes smooth and elastic.
Place the dough in a lightly oiled bowl, cover it with a damp cloth, and let it rise in a warm place for 1-2 hours or until it doubles in size.
Grease a loaf pan with butter.
Punch down the risen dough and turn it onto a floured surface. Shape it into a rectangle that fits the size of your loaf pan.
Place the shaped dough into the greased loaf pan, cover it with a damp cloth, and let it rise for an additional 30-45 minutes.
Preheat your oven to 180°C (350°F).
Bake the Pain de Mie in the preheated oven for 30-35 minutes or until the top is golden brown, and the bread sounds hollow when tapped.
Allow the bread to cool in the pan for a few minutes before transferring it to a wire rack to cool completely.

Pain de Mie is a versatile bread perfect for sandwiches or toasting. Enjoy your homemade Pain de Mie!

**Pain Complet**

Ingredients:

- 400g whole wheat flour
- 100g all-purpose flour
- 350ml lukewarm water
- 10g salt
- 7g active dry yeast
- 1 tablespoon honey or molasses (optional, for sweetness)

Instructions:

In a small bowl, combine the lukewarm water with honey (or molasses) and sprinkle the active dry yeast over it. Allow it to sit for 5-10 minutes until the mixture becomes frothy.
In a large mixing bowl, combine the whole wheat flour, all-purpose flour, and salt.
Make a well in the center of the flour mixture and pour the activated yeast mixture into it.
Gradually incorporate the flour into the liquid, stirring with a wooden spoon or your hands until a dough forms.
Knead the dough on a floured surface for about 10-15 minutes until it is smooth and elastic.
Place the dough in a lightly oiled bowl, cover it with a damp cloth, and let it rise in a warm place for 1-2 hours or until it doubles in size.
Preheat your oven to 190°C (375°F).
Punch down the risen dough and turn it onto a floured surface. Shape it into a round or oval loaf.
Place the shaped dough on a parchment-lined or floured baking sheet.
Allow the bread to rest for an additional 15-20 minutes.
Bake in the preheated oven for 35-40 minutes or until the crust is golden brown, and the bread sounds hollow when tapped.
Cool the Pain Complet on a wire rack before slicing.

Enjoy your homemade Pain Complet, a wholesome whole wheat bread that's perfect for a variety of uses!

## Pain Poilâne

Ingredients:

- 400g bread flour
- 100g whole wheat flour
- 350ml lukewarm water
- 10g salt
- 7g active dry yeast
- 1 tablespoon honey
- 2 tablespoons wheat bran
- 2 tablespoons cornmeal (for dusting)

Instructions:

In a small bowl, combine the lukewarm water and honey. Sprinkle the active dry yeast over the mixture, stir gently, and let it sit for 5-10 minutes until frothy.
In a large mixing bowl, combine the bread flour, whole wheat flour, and salt. Add wheat bran to the mixture.
Make a well in the center of the flour mixture and pour the activated yeast mixture into it.
Gradually incorporate the flour into the liquid, stirring with a wooden spoon or your hands until a dough forms.
Knead the dough on a floured surface for about 10-15 minutes until it is smooth and elastic.
Place the dough in a lightly oiled bowl, cover it with a damp cloth, and let it rise in a warm place for 1-2 hours or until it doubles in size.
Preheat your oven to 220°C (425°F).
Punch down the risen dough and turn it onto a floured surface. Shape it into a round or oval loaf.
Dust a baking sheet with cornmeal and place the shaped dough on it.
Allow the bread to rest for an additional 15-20 minutes.
Using a sharp knife, make a crosshatch pattern on the top of the bread.
Bake in the preheated oven for 30-35 minutes or until the crust is golden brown, and the bread sounds hollow when tapped.
Cool the Pain Poilâne on a wire rack before slicing.

Pain Poilâne is known for its distinctive crosshatch pattern and rustic flavor. Enjoy this delicious bread as part of your meals!

**Pain Viennois**

Ingredients:

- 500g bread flour
- 80g sugar
- 10g salt
- 10g active dry yeast
- 300ml lukewarm milk
- 100g unsalted butter, softened
- 1 egg (for egg wash)
- Pearl sugar (optional, for topping)

Instructions:

In a small bowl, combine lukewarm milk and sugar. Stir until the sugar is dissolved. Sprinkle the active dry yeast over the mixture, give it a gentle stir, and let it sit for 5-10 minutes until frothy.
In a large mixing bowl, combine the bread flour and salt.
Create a well in the center of the flour mixture and pour the activated yeast mixture into it.
Gradually incorporate the flour into the liquid, mixing with a wooden spoon or your hands until a dough forms.
Knead the dough on a floured surface for about 10-15 minutes until it becomes smooth and elastic.
Place the dough in a lightly oiled bowl, cover it with a damp cloth, and let it rise in a warm place for 1-2 hours or until it doubles in size.
Preheat your oven to 180°C (350°F).
Punch down the risen dough and turn it onto a floured surface. Roll it into a rectangle.
Spread the softened butter over the surface of the dough.
Roll the dough into a log and place it in a greased loaf pan.
Beat the egg and brush it over the top of the dough. Sprinkle pearl sugar on top if desired.
Allow the dough to rise for an additional 30-45 minutes.
Bake in the preheated oven for 25-30 minutes or until the top is golden brown and the bread sounds hollow when tapped.
Cool the Pain Viennois in the pan for a few minutes before transferring it to a wire rack to cool completely.

This Pain Viennois is a sweet and rich bread, perfect for breakfast or as a delightful snack. Enjoy!

**Pain de Seigle**

Ingredients:

- 300g rye flour
- 200g bread flour
- 10g salt
- 7g active dry yeast
- 300ml lukewarm water
- 1 tablespoon molasses or honey (optional, for sweetness)
- 1 tablespoon caraway seeds (optional, for flavor)

Instructions:

In a small bowl, combine the lukewarm water and molasses (or honey). Sprinkle the active dry yeast over the mixture, stir gently, and let it sit for 5-10 minutes until frothy.
In a large mixing bowl, combine the rye flour, bread flour, and salt. Add caraway seeds if desired.
Create a well in the center of the flour mixture and pour the activated yeast mixture into it.
Gradually incorporate the flour into the liquid, mixing with a wooden spoon or your hands until a dough forms.
Knead the dough on a floured surface for about 10-15 minutes until it is smooth and elastic.
Place the dough in a lightly oiled bowl, cover it with a damp cloth, and let it rise in a warm place for 1-2 hours or until it doubles in size.
Preheat your oven to 200°C (400°F).
Punch down the risen dough and shape it into a round or oval loaf.
Place the shaped dough on a parchment-lined or floured baking sheet.
Allow the bread to rest for an additional 15-20 minutes.
Using a sharp knife, make a few slashes on the top of the bread to allow for expansion during baking.
Bake in the preheated oven for 35-40 minutes or until the crust is golden brown, and the bread sounds hollow when tapped.
Cool the Pain de Seigle on a wire rack before slicing.

Enjoy your homemade Pain de Seigle, a hearty and flavorful rye bread that goes well with a variety of toppings or as an accompaniment to soups and stews!

**Pain de Noix**

Ingredients:

- 400g bread flour
- 100g whole wheat flour
- 10g salt
- 7g active dry yeast
- 300ml lukewarm water
- 50g unsalted butter, softened
- 100g walnuts, chopped

Instructions:

In a small bowl, combine the lukewarm water and active dry yeast. Allow it to sit for 5-10 minutes until the mixture becomes frothy.
In a large mixing bowl, combine the bread flour, whole wheat flour, and salt.
Make a well in the center of the flour mixture and pour the activated yeast mixture into it.
Gradually incorporate the flour into the liquid, stirring with a wooden spoon or your hands until a dough forms.
Knead the dough on a floured surface for about 10-15 minutes until it is smooth and elastic.
Incorporate the softened butter into the dough, kneading until it is well combined.
Fold in the chopped walnuts and continue kneading until they are evenly distributed throughout the dough.
Place the dough in a lightly oiled bowl, cover it with a damp cloth, and let it rise in a warm place for 1-2 hours or until it doubles in size.
Preheat your oven to 200°C (400°F).
Punch down the risen dough and shape it into a round or oval loaf.
Place the shaped dough on a parchment-lined or floured baking sheet.
Allow the bread to rest for an additional 15-20 minutes.
Bake in the preheated oven for 35-40 minutes or until the crust is golden brown, and the bread sounds hollow when tapped.
Cool the Pain de Noix on a wire rack before slicing.

This Pain de Noix is a delightful bread with the rich flavor of walnuts, making it a great choice for both sweet and savory pairings. Enjoy!

**Pain de Céréales**

Ingredients:

- 400g bread flour
- 100g whole wheat flour
- 50g rye flour
- 10g salt
- 7g active dry yeast
- 300ml lukewarm water
- 2 tablespoons honey or molasses
- 3 tablespoons mixed seeds (such as sunflower, flax, and sesame)
- 3 tablespoons rolled oats

Instructions:

In a small bowl, combine the lukewarm water and honey (or molasses). Sprinkle the active dry yeast over the mixture, stir gently, and let it sit for 5-10 minutes until frothy.
In a large mixing bowl, combine the bread flour, whole wheat flour, rye flour, and salt.
Create a well in the center of the flour mixture and pour the activated yeast mixture into it.
Gradually incorporate the flour into the liquid, mixing with a wooden spoon or your hands until a dough forms.
Knead the dough on a floured surface for about 10-15 minutes until it is smooth and elastic.
Place the dough in a lightly oiled bowl, cover it with a damp cloth, and let it rise in a warm place for 1-2 hours or until it doubles in size.
Preheat your oven to 200°C (400°F).
Punch down the risen dough and turn it onto a floured surface. Shape it into a round or oval loaf.
Mix the mixed seeds and rolled oats together and press them onto the surface of the dough.
Place the shaped dough on a parchment-lined or floured baking sheet.
Allow the bread to rest for an additional 15-20 minutes.
Using a sharp knife, make a few slashes on the top of the bread.

Bake in the preheated oven for 35-40 minutes or until the crust is golden brown, and the bread sounds hollow when tapped.

Cool the Pain de Céréales on a wire rack before slicing.

Enjoy your homemade Pain de Céréales, a wholesome multigrain bread that's perfect for sandwiches or toasting!

**Pain d'Épices Baguette**

Ingredients:

- 400g all-purpose flour
- 100g rye flour
- 10g baking powder
- 5g ground cinnamon
- 5g ground ginger
- 2g ground cloves
- 1/2 teaspoon salt
- 300ml whole milk
- 150g honey
- 50g unsalted butter, melted
- 50g candied orange peel, finely chopped (optional)

Instructions:

Preheat your oven to 180°C (350°F). Line a baking sheet with parchment paper.
In a large mixing bowl, combine the all-purpose flour, rye flour, baking powder, ground cinnamon, ground ginger, ground cloves, and salt.
In a separate saucepan, warm the whole milk over low heat. Add honey and melted butter to the warm milk, stirring until well combined.
Make a well in the center of the dry ingredients and pour the wet ingredients into it. Mix until a dough forms.
Fold in the candied orange peel, if using.
Turn the dough onto a floured surface and knead it for about 5-7 minutes until it becomes smooth and elastic.
Shape the dough into a baguette form and place it on the prepared baking sheet.
Bake in the preheated oven for 25-30 minutes or until the top is golden brown and the bread sounds hollow when tapped.
Allow the Pain d'Épices Baguette to cool on a wire rack before slicing.

This Pain d'Épices Baguette is a delightful combination of spices and honey, making it a unique and flavorful bread. Enjoy it as is or with a spread of butter!

**Pain aux Noix et Raisins**

Ingredients:

- 400g bread flour
- 100g whole wheat flour
- 10g salt
- 7g active dry yeast
- 300ml lukewarm water
- 50g unsalted butter, softened
- 100g walnuts, chopped
- 100g raisins

Instructions:

In a small bowl, combine the lukewarm water and active dry yeast. Allow it to sit for 5-10 minutes until the mixture becomes frothy.
In a large mixing bowl, combine the bread flour, whole wheat flour, and salt.
Make a well in the center of the flour mixture and pour the activated yeast mixture into it.
Gradually incorporate the flour into the liquid, stirring with a wooden spoon or your hands until a dough forms.
Knead the dough on a floured surface for about 10-15 minutes until it is smooth and elastic.
Incorporate the softened butter into the dough, kneading until it is well combined.
Fold in the chopped walnuts and raisins, ensuring an even distribution throughout the dough.
Place the dough in a lightly oiled bowl, cover it with a damp cloth, and let it rise in a warm place for 1-2 hours or until it doubles in size.
Preheat your oven to 200°C (400°F).
Punch down the risen dough and shape it into a round or oval loaf.
Place the shaped dough on a parchment-lined or floured baking sheet.
Allow the bread to rest for an additional 15-20 minutes.
Using a sharp knife, make a few slashes on the top of the bread to allow for expansion during baking.
Bake in the preheated oven for 35-40 minutes or until the crust is golden brown, and the bread sounds hollow when tapped.
Cool the Pain aux Noix et Raisins on a wire rack before slicing.

Enjoy this delicious Pain aux Noix et Raisins, a delightful combination of the nuttiness of walnuts and the sweetness of raisins in every bite!

**Pain aux Olives**

Ingredients:

- 500g bread flour
- 10g salt
- 7g active dry yeast
- 300ml lukewarm water
- 3 tablespoons olive oil
- 200g pitted black or green olives, chopped
- 1 tablespoon dried oregano (optional)
- 1 tablespoon dried thyme (optional)

Instructions:

In a small bowl, combine the lukewarm water and active dry yeast. Allow it to sit for 5-10 minutes until the mixture becomes frothy.
In a large mixing bowl, combine the bread flour and salt.
Make a well in the center of the flour mixture and pour the activated yeast mixture into it.
Gradually incorporate the flour into the liquid, stirring with a wooden spoon or your hands until a dough forms.
Knead the dough on a floured surface for about 10-15 minutes until it is smooth and elastic.
Place the dough in a lightly oiled bowl, cover it with a damp cloth, and let it rise in a warm place for 1-2 hours or until it doubles in size.
Preheat your oven to 200°C (400°F).
Punch down the risen dough and turn it onto a floured surface. Flatten the dough and sprinkle the chopped olives evenly over it.
Fold and knead the dough to distribute the olives evenly throughout.
Shape the dough into a round or oval loaf and place it on a parchment-lined or floured baking sheet.
Optional: Sprinkle dried oregano and thyme on top of the loaf, pressing them slightly into the dough.
Allow the bread to rest for an additional 15-20 minutes.
Using a sharp knife, make a few slashes on the top of the bread.
Bake in the preheated oven for 30-35 minutes or until the crust is golden brown, and the bread sounds hollow when tapped.

Cool the Pain aux Olives on a wire rack before slicing.

Enjoy your homemade Pain aux Olives, a flavorful bread that pairs wonderfully with cheese or can be enjoyed on its own!

**Pain de Provence**

Ingredients:

- 500g bread flour
- 10g salt
- 7g active dry yeast
- 300ml lukewarm water
- 3 tablespoons olive oil
- 1 tablespoon herbes de Provence (a blend of dried herbs like rosemary, thyme, oregano, savory, and marjoram)
- 1 teaspoon dried lavender flowers (optional)

Instructions:

In a small bowl, combine the lukewarm water and active dry yeast. Allow it to sit for 5-10 minutes until the mixture becomes frothy.
In a large mixing bowl, combine the bread flour and salt.
Make a well in the center of the flour mixture and pour the activated yeast mixture into it.
Gradually incorporate the flour into the liquid, stirring with a wooden spoon or your hands until a dough forms.
Knead the dough on a floured surface for about 10-15 minutes until it is smooth and elastic.
Place the dough in a lightly oiled bowl, cover it with a damp cloth, and let it rise in a warm place for 1-2 hours or until it doubles in size.
Preheat your oven to 200°C (400°F).
Punch down the risen dough and turn it onto a floured surface. Flatten the dough and sprinkle the herbes de Provence evenly over it.
Fold and knead the dough to distribute the herbs evenly throughout.
Shape the dough into a round or oval loaf and place it on a parchment-lined or floured baking sheet.
Optional: Sprinkle dried lavender flowers on top of the loaf, pressing them slightly into the dough.
Allow the bread to rest for an additional 15-20 minutes.
Using a sharp knife, make a few slashes on the top of the bread.
Bake in the preheated oven for 30-35 minutes or until the crust is golden brown, and the bread sounds hollow when tapped.

Cool the Pain de Provence on a wire rack before slicing.

Enjoy your homemade Pain de Provence, a fragrant and herby bread inspired by the flavors of the Provence region in France!

**Pain de Petit Épeautre**

Ingredients:

- 400g einkorn flour
- 100g bread flour
- 10g salt
- 7g active dry yeast
- 300ml lukewarm water
- 3 tablespoons olive oil

Instructions:

In a small bowl, combine the lukewarm water and active dry yeast. Allow it to sit for 5-10 minutes until the mixture becomes frothy.
In a large mixing bowl, combine the einkorn flour, bread flour, and salt.
Make a well in the center of the flour mixture and pour the activated yeast mixture into it.
Gradually incorporate the flour into the liquid, stirring with a wooden spoon or your hands until a dough forms.
Knead the dough on a floured surface for about 10-15 minutes until it is smooth and elastic.
Place the dough in a lightly oiled bowl, cover it with a damp cloth, and let it rise in a warm place for 1-2 hours or until it doubles in size.
Preheat your oven to 200°C (400°F).
Punch down the risen dough and turn it onto a floured surface.
Shape the dough into a round or oval loaf and place it on a parchment-lined or floured baking sheet.
Drizzle olive oil over the top of the loaf, spreading it evenly.
Allow the bread to rest for an additional 15-20 minutes.
Using a sharp knife, make a few slashes on the top of the bread.
Bake in the preheated oven for 30-35 minutes or until the crust is golden brown, and the bread sounds hollow when tapped.
Cool the Pain de Petit Épeautre on a wire rack before slicing.

Einkorn flour has a distinct nutty flavor, and this bread is a wonderful showcase for it. Enjoy your homemade Pain de Petit Épeautre!

**Pain de Sarrasin**

Ingredients:

- 300g buckwheat flour
- 200g all-purpose flour
- 10g salt
- 7g active dry yeast
- 300ml lukewarm water
- 3 tablespoons olive oil

Instructions:

In a small bowl, combine the lukewarm water and active dry yeast. Allow it to sit for 5-10 minutes until the mixture becomes frothy.
In a large mixing bowl, combine the buckwheat flour, all-purpose flour, and salt.
Make a well in the center of the flour mixture and pour the activated yeast mixture into it.
Gradually incorporate the flour into the liquid, stirring with a wooden spoon or your hands until a dough forms.
Knead the dough on a floured surface for about 10-15 minutes until it is smooth and elastic.
Place the dough in a lightly oiled bowl, cover it with a damp cloth, and let it rise in a warm place for 1-2 hours or until it doubles in size.
Preheat your oven to 200°C (400°F).
Punch down the risen dough and turn it onto a floured surface.
Shape the dough into a round or oval loaf and place it on a parchment-lined or floured baking sheet.
Drizzle olive oil over the top of the loaf, spreading it evenly.
Allow the bread to rest for an additional 15-20 minutes.
Using a sharp knife, make a few slashes on the top of the bread.
Bake in the preheated oven for 30-35 minutes or until the crust is golden brown, and the bread sounds hollow when tapped.
Cool the Pain de Sarrasin on a wire rack before slicing.

Buckwheat flour gives this bread a unique flavor and a hearty texture. Enjoy your homemade Pain de Sarrasin!

**Pain aux Fruits Secs**

Ingredients:

- 500g bread flour
- 10g salt
- 7g active dry yeast
- 300ml lukewarm water
- 3 tablespoons olive oil
- 200g mixed dried fruits (such as raisins, currants, apricots, and figs), chopped
- 1 tablespoon honey or maple syrup (optional, for sweetness)

Instructions:

In a small bowl, combine the lukewarm water and active dry yeast. Allow it to sit for 5-10 minutes until the mixture becomes frothy.
In a large mixing bowl, combine the bread flour and salt.
Make a well in the center of the flour mixture and pour the activated yeast mixture into it.
Gradually incorporate the flour into the liquid, stirring with a wooden spoon or your hands until a dough forms.
Knead the dough on a floured surface for about 10-15 minutes until it is smooth and elastic.
Place the dough in a lightly oiled bowl, cover it with a damp cloth, and let it rise in a warm place for 1-2 hours or until it doubles in size.
Preheat your oven to 200°C (400°F).
Punch down the risen dough and turn it onto a floured surface.
Sprinkle the chopped dried fruits over the dough and knead it to distribute the fruits evenly.
Shape the dough into a round or oval loaf and place it on a parchment-lined or floured baking sheet.
Drizzle olive oil over the top of the loaf, spreading it evenly.
Optional: Drizzle honey or maple syrup over the top of the loaf for added sweetness.
Allow the bread to rest for an additional 15-20 minutes.
Using a sharp knife, make a few slashes on the top of the bread.
Bake in the preheated oven for 30-35 minutes or until the crust is golden brown, and the bread sounds hollow when tapped.
Cool the Pain aux Fruits Secs on a wire rack before slicing.

Enjoy your homemade Dried Fruit Bread, a sweet and hearty treat perfect for breakfast or as a snack!

**Pain de Courgettes**

Ingredients:

- 2 cups shredded zucchini (about 2 medium-sized zucchinis)
- 3 cups all-purpose flour
- 1 teaspoon baking powder
- 1/2 teaspoon baking soda
- 1/2 teaspoon salt
- 1 teaspoon ground cinnamon
- 1/2 teaspoon ground nutmeg
- 3/4 cup granulated sugar
- 1/2 cup brown sugar, packed
- 1/2 cup vegetable oil
- 3 large eggs
- 1 teaspoon vanilla extract
- 1/2 cup chopped nuts or chocolate chips (optional)

Instructions:

Preheat your oven to 350°F (175°C). Grease and flour a 9x5-inch loaf pan.
Shred the zucchini using a grater. Place the shredded zucchini in a clean kitchen towel and squeeze out any excess moisture.
In a large bowl, whisk together the flour, baking powder, baking soda, salt, cinnamon, and nutmeg.
In another bowl, whisk together the granulated sugar, brown sugar, vegetable oil, eggs, and vanilla extract until well combined.
Add the shredded zucchini to the wet ingredients and mix well.
Gradually add the dry ingredients to the wet ingredients, stirring until just combined. Do not overmix.
If using, fold in the chopped nuts or chocolate chips.
Pour the batter into the prepared loaf pan, spreading it evenly.
Bake in the preheated oven for 50-60 minutes or until a toothpick inserted into the center comes out clean.
Allow the Pain de Courgettes to cool in the pan for 10 minutes before transferring it to a wire rack to cool completely.
Once cooled, slice and serve. Enjoy your Zucchini Bread!

This Pain de Courgettes (Zucchini Bread) is a moist and delicious treat, perfect for breakfast or a snack. Feel free to customize it by adding your favorite mix-ins like nuts or chocolate chips!

## Pain au Levain Naturel

Ingredients:

- 500g bread flour
- 100g whole wheat flour
- 10g salt
- 300g active sourdough starter (100% hydration)
- 350-400ml lukewarm water

Instructions:

In a large mixing bowl, combine the bread flour, whole wheat flour, and salt.
Add the active sourdough starter to the flour mixture.
Gradually add lukewarm water to the mixture, stirring with a wooden spoon or your hands, until a dough forms. Adjust the water amount as needed to achieve a soft and slightly sticky dough.
Knead the dough on a floured surface for about 10-15 minutes until it is smooth and elastic.
Place the dough in a lightly oiled bowl, cover it with a damp cloth, and let it rest for 4-6 hours, allowing it to undergo bulk fermentation. During this time, perform stretch and folds every 30 minutes for the first 2 hours.
After bulk fermentation, shape the dough into a round or oval loaf and place it in a well-floured proofing basket.
Cover the basket with a cloth and let the dough undergo final proofing for 2-4 hours or until it has visibly increased in size.
Preheat your oven to 230°C (450°F). If you have a baking stone, place it in the oven during preheating.
Optional: Slash the top of the dough with a sharp knife or razor blade to create a decorative pattern.
If using a baking stone, carefully transfer the dough onto the hot stone.
Otherwise, place the dough on a parchment-lined baking sheet.
Bake in the preheated oven for 30-40 minutes or until the crust is deep golden brown and the bread sounds hollow when tapped on the bottom.
Cool the Pain au Levain Naturel on a wire rack before slicing.

Enjoy your homemade Sourdough Bread with a delightful crust and tangy flavor from the natural fermentation of the sourdough starter!

## Pain à l'Ancienne

Ingredients:

- 500g bread flour
- 10g salt
- 7g active dry yeast
- 375ml cold water
- 2 tablespoons olive oil

Instructions:

In a large mixing bowl, combine the bread flour and salt.

In a small bowl, dissolve the active dry yeast in cold water. Let it sit for a couple of minutes until it starts to foam.

Add the yeast mixture to the flour and mix until a shaggy dough forms.

Drizzle olive oil over the dough and mix it in, kneading lightly until the dough comes together.

Cover the bowl with plastic wrap and let the dough rest in the refrigerator for at least 8-24 hours. This slow fermentation enhances the flavor of the bread.

After the resting period, preheat your oven to 230°C (450°F).

Turn the dough out onto a floured surface and shape it into a round or oval loaf.

Place the shaped dough on a parchment-lined or floured baking sheet.

Allow the bread to rest for an additional 30-60 minutes.

Optional: Slash the top of the dough with a sharp knife or razor blade to allow for expansion during baking.

Bake in the preheated oven for 25-30 minutes or until the crust is golden brown and the bread sounds hollow when tapped on the bottom.

Cool the Pain à l'Ancienne on a wire rack before slicing.

This Pain à l'Ancienne is characterized by its rustic appearance and enhanced flavor due to the extended fermentation. Enjoy this simple yet delicious bread!

**Pain de Maïs**

Ingredients:

- 1 cup cornmeal
- 1 cup all-purpose flour
- 1 tablespoon baking powder
- 1/2 teaspoon salt
- 2 tablespoons sugar (adjust to taste)
- 1 cup buttermilk
- 2 large eggs
- 1/4 cup unsalted butter, melted
- 1/4 cup vegetable oil

Instructions:

Preheat your oven to 200°C (400°F). Grease a 9-inch square baking pan or a cast-iron skillet.
In a large mixing bowl, whisk together the cornmeal, all-purpose flour, baking powder, salt, and sugar.
In another bowl, whisk together the buttermilk, eggs, melted butter, and vegetable oil.
Pour the wet ingredients into the dry ingredients and stir until just combined. Do not overmix; a few lumps are okay.
Pour the batter into the prepared baking pan or skillet.
Bake in the preheated oven for 20-25 minutes or until the top is golden brown and a toothpick inserted into the center comes out clean.
Allow the Pain de Maïs to cool in the pan for a few minutes before transferring it to a wire rack to cool completely.
Slice and serve. Enjoy your Cornbread!

Cornbread is a versatile and delicious addition to meals, and this Pain de Maïs recipe is easy to make. It's perfect as a side dish, for breakfast, or with chili. Adjust the sugar quantity based on your preference for sweetness.

**Pain de Lentilles**

Ingredients:

- 1 cup cooked lentils, cooled
- 3 cups bread flour
- 1 cup whole wheat flour
- 10g salt
- 7g active dry yeast
- 1 1/2 cups lukewarm water
- 2 tablespoons olive oil

Instructions:

In a blender or food processor, puree the cooked lentils with a little water until you have a smooth consistency. Set aside.
In a large mixing bowl, combine the bread flour, whole wheat flour, and salt.
In a small bowl, mix the lukewarm water and active dry yeast. Allow it to sit for 5-10 minutes until it becomes frothy.
Add the lentil puree and olive oil to the yeast mixture.
Make a well in the center of the flour mixture and pour the wet ingredients into it.
Gradually incorporate the flour into the liquid, stirring with a wooden spoon or your hands until a dough forms.
Knead the dough on a floured surface for about 10-15 minutes until it is smooth and elastic.
Place the dough in a lightly oiled bowl, cover it with a damp cloth, and let it rise in a warm place for 1-2 hours or until it doubles in size.
Preheat your oven to 200°C (400°F).
Punch down the risen dough and turn it onto a floured surface.
Shape the dough into a round or oval loaf and place it on a parchment-lined or floured baking sheet.
Allow the bread to rest for an additional 15-20 minutes.
Using a sharp knife, make a few slashes on the top of the bread.
Bake in the preheated oven for 30-35 minutes or until the crust is golden brown, and the bread sounds hollow when tapped.
Cool the Pain de Lentilles on a wire rack before slicing.

Enjoy your homemade Lentil Bread, a nutritious and flavorful alternative to traditional bread!

**Pain de Quinoa**

Ingredients:

- 1 cup quinoa, rinsed and cooked
- 2 cups bread flour
- 1 cup whole wheat flour
- 10g salt
- 7g active dry yeast
- 1 1/2 cups lukewarm water
- 2 tablespoons olive oil

Instructions:

In a blender or food processor, puree the cooked quinoa with a little water until you have a smooth consistency. Set aside.
In a large mixing bowl, combine the bread flour, whole wheat flour, and salt.
In a small bowl, mix the lukewarm water and active dry yeast. Allow it to sit for 5-10 minutes until it becomes frothy.
Add the quinoa puree and olive oil to the yeast mixture.
Make a well in the center of the flour mixture and pour the wet ingredients into it. Gradually incorporate the flour into the liquid, stirring with a wooden spoon or your hands until a dough forms.
Knead the dough on a floured surface for about 10-15 minutes until it is smooth and elastic.
Place the dough in a lightly oiled bowl, cover it with a damp cloth, and let it rise in a warm place for 1-2 hours or until it doubles in size.
Preheat your oven to 200°C (400°F).
Punch down the risen dough and turn it onto a floured surface.
Shape the dough into a round or oval loaf and place it on a parchment-lined or floured baking sheet.
Allow the bread to rest for an additional 15-20 minutes.
Using a sharp knife, make a few slashes on the top of the bread.
Bake in the preheated oven for 30-35 minutes or until the crust is golden brown, and the bread sounds hollow when tapped.
Cool the Pain de Quinoa on a wire rack before slicing.

Enjoy your homemade Quinoa Bread, a nutritious and hearty option with the added benefits of quinoa!

**Pain de Tomates Séchées**

Ingredients:

- 500g bread flour
- 10g salt
- 7g active dry yeast
- 1 cup warm water
- 2 tablespoons olive oil
- 1/2 cup sun-dried tomatoes, chopped (drained if packed in oil)
- 1 tablespoon dried basil
- 1 tablespoon dried oregano

Instructions:

In a small bowl, dissolve the active dry yeast in warm water. Let it sit for 5-10 minutes until it becomes frothy.
In a large mixing bowl, combine the bread flour and salt.
Make a well in the center of the flour mixture and pour the activated yeast mixture into it.
Gradually incorporate the flour into the liquid, stirring with a wooden spoon or your hands until a dough forms.
Knead the dough on a floured surface for about 10-15 minutes until it is smooth and elastic.
Place the dough in a lightly oiled bowl, cover it with a damp cloth, and let it rise in a warm place for 1-2 hours or until it doubles in size.
Preheat your oven to 200°C (400°F).
Punch down the risen dough and turn it onto a floured surface.
Flatten the dough and spread the chopped sun-dried tomatoes evenly over it.
Sprinkle the dried basil and oregano on top.
Fold and knead the dough to distribute the tomatoes and herbs evenly throughout.
Shape the dough into a round or oval loaf and place it on a parchment-lined or floured baking sheet.
Allow the bread to rest for an additional 15-20 minutes.
Using a sharp knife, make a few slashes on the top of the bread.
Bake in the preheated oven for 30-35 minutes or until the crust is golden brown, and the bread sounds hollow when tapped.

Cool the Pain de Tomates Séchées on a wire rack before slicing.

Enjoy your homemade Sun-Dried Tomato Bread, a flavorful and savory option for various meals and occasions!

**Pain aux Herbes de Provence**

Ingredients:

- 500g bread flour
- 10g salt
- 7g active dry yeast
- 300ml lukewarm water
- 3 tablespoons olive oil
- 1 tablespoon herbes de Provence (a blend of dried herbs like rosemary, thyme, oregano, savory, and marjoram)

Instructions:

In a small bowl, combine the lukewarm water and active dry yeast. Allow it to sit for 5-10 minutes until the mixture becomes frothy.
In a large mixing bowl, combine the bread flour and salt.
Make a well in the center of the flour mixture and pour the activated yeast mixture into it.
Gradually incorporate the flour into the liquid, stirring with a wooden spoon or your hands until a dough forms.
Knead the dough on a floured surface for about 10-15 minutes until it is smooth and elastic.
Place the dough in a lightly oiled bowl, cover it with a damp cloth, and let it rise in a warm place for 1-2 hours or until it doubles in size.
Preheat your oven to 200°C (400°F).
Punch down the risen dough and turn it onto a floured surface.
Flatten the dough and sprinkle the herbes de Provence evenly over it.
Fold and knead the dough to distribute the herbs evenly throughout.
Shape the dough into a round or oval loaf and place it on a parchment-lined or floured baking sheet.
Allow the bread to rest for an additional 15-20 minutes.
Using a sharp knife, make a few slashes on the top of the bread.
Bake in the preheated oven for 30-35 minutes or until the crust is golden brown, and the bread sounds hollow when tapped.
Cool the Pain aux Herbes de Provence on a wire rack before slicing.

Enjoy the delightful flavors of Provence with this herb-infused bread! Serve it as a side to meals or with olive oil for dipping.

**Pain aux Figues**

Ingredients:

- 500g bread flour
- 10g salt
- 7g active dry yeast
- 300ml lukewarm water
- 3 tablespoons olive oil
- 200g dried figs, chopped
- 1 tablespoon honey

Instructions:

In a small bowl, combine the lukewarm water and active dry yeast. Allow it to sit for 5-10 minutes until the mixture becomes frothy.
In a large mixing bowl, combine the bread flour and salt.
Make a well in the center of the flour mixture and pour the activated yeast mixture into it.
Gradually incorporate the flour into the liquid, stirring with a wooden spoon or your hands until a dough forms.
Knead the dough on a floured surface for about 10-15 minutes until it is smooth and elastic.
Place the dough in a lightly oiled bowl, cover it with a damp cloth, and let it rise in a warm place for 1-2 hours or until it doubles in size.
Preheat your oven to 200°C (400°F).
Punch down the risen dough and turn it onto a floured surface.
Flatten the dough and sprinkle the chopped dried figs evenly over it.
Drizzle honey over the figs.
Fold and knead the dough to distribute the figs and honey evenly throughout.
Shape the dough into a round or oval loaf and place it on a parchment-lined or floured baking sheet.
Allow the bread to rest for an additional 15-20 minutes.
Using a sharp knife, make a few slashes on the top of the bread.
Bake in the preheated oven for 30-35 minutes or until the crust is golden brown, and the bread sounds hollow when tapped.
Cool the Pain aux Figues on a wire rack before slicing.

Enjoy the sweetness of figs in every bite with this delicious Fig Bread. It pairs well with cheese or makes for a tasty breakfast option!

**Pain à l'Ail**

Ingredients:

- 1 loaf of French or Italian bread
- 1/2 cup (1 stick) unsalted butter, softened
- 4-6 cloves garlic, minced
- 2 tablespoons fresh parsley, finely chopped
- Salt to taste

Instructions:

Preheat your oven to 180°C (350°F).
In a small bowl, combine the softened butter, minced garlic, chopped parsley, and salt. Mix well until the ingredients are evenly incorporated.
Slice the loaf of French or Italian bread in half lengthwise.
Spread the garlic butter mixture evenly over the cut sides of the bread.
Place the bread on a baking sheet and bake in the preheated oven for 10-15 minutes or until the edges are golden brown and the garlic is fragrant.
Optionally, you can broil the bread for an additional 1-2 minutes to get a slight y crispy top.
Remove the garlic bread from the oven and let it cool for a few minutes.
Slice the bread into individual servings and serve warm.

Garlic Bread is a perfect accompaniment to pasta dishes, soups, or as a side for various meals. Enjoy the rich garlic and butter flavors in every bite!

**Pain de Champagne**

Ingredients:

- 500g bread flour
- 10g salt
- 7g active dry yeast
- 300ml lukewarm water
- 3 tablespoons olive oil
- 1/4 cup Champagne or sparkling wine

Instructions:

In a small bowl, combine the lukewarm water and active dry yeast. Allow it to sit for 5-10 minutes until the mixture becomes frothy.
In a large mixing bowl, combine the bread flour and salt.
Make a well in the center of the flour mixture and pour the activated yeast mixture into it.
Add the olive oil and Champagne to the well.
Gradually incorporate the flour into the liquid, stirring with a wooden spoon or your hands until a dough forms.
Knead the dough on a floured surface for about 10-15 minutes until it is smooth and elastic.
Place the dough in a lightly oiled bowl, cover it with a damp cloth, and let it rise in a warm place for 1-2 hours or until it doubles in size.
Preheat your oven to 200°C (400°F).
Punch down the risen dough and turn it onto a floured surface.
Shape the dough into a round or oval loaf and place it on a parchment-lined or floured baking sheet.
Allow the bread to rest for an additional 15-20 minutes.
Using a sharp knife, make a few slashes on the top of the bread.
Bake in the preheated oven for 30-35 minutes or until the crust is golden brown, and the bread sounds hollow when tapped.
Cool the Pain de Champagne on a wire rack before slicing.

Enjoy your homemade Champagne Bread with a unique touch of bubbly flavor! It's a delightful choice for special occasions or when you want to add a touch of sophistication to your bread.

**Pain au Fromage**

Ingredients:

- 500g bread flour
- 10g salt
- 7g active dry yeast
- 300ml lukewarm water
- 3 tablespoons olive oil
- 200g grated cheese (cheddar, Gruyère, or your choice)
- 1/4 cup finely chopped fresh herbs (such as parsley or chives)

Instructions:

In a small bowl, combine the lukewarm water and active dry yeast. Allow it to sit for 5-10 minutes until the mixture becomes frothy.
In a large mixing bowl, combine the bread flour and salt.
Make a well in the center of the flour mixture and pour the activated yeast mixture into it.
Add the olive oil, grated cheese, and chopped herbs to the well.
Gradually incorporate the flour into the liquid, stirring with a wooden spoon or your hands until a dough forms.
Knead the dough on a floured surface for about 10-15 minutes until it is smooth and elastic.
Place the dough in a lightly oiled bowl, cover it with a damp cloth, and let it rise in a warm place for 1-2 hours or until it doubles in size.
Preheat your oven to 200°C (400°F).
Punch down the risen dough and turn it onto a floured surface.
Shape the dough into a round or oval loaf and place it on a parchment-lined or floured baking sheet.
Allow the bread to rest for an additional 15-20 minutes.
Using a sharp knife, make a few slashes on the top of the bread.
Bake in the preheated oven for 30-35 minutes or until the crust is golden brown, and the bread sounds hollow when tapped.
Cool the Pain au Fromage on a wire rack before slicing.

Enjoy your homemade Cheese Bread with the delicious combination of melted cheese and fresh herbs! It's a savory treat perfect for serving on its own or alongside soups and salads.

**Pain à la Bière**

Ingredients:

- 500g all-purpose flour
- 10g salt
- 7g active dry yeast
- 300ml lukewarm beer (room temperature)
- 3 tablespoons olive oil
- 1 tablespoon sugar (optional, for a slightly sweeter flavor)

Instructions:

In a small bowl, combine the lukewarm beer and active dry yeast. Allow it to sit for 5-10 minutes until the mixture becomes frothy.
In a large mixing bowl, combine the all-purpose flour and salt.
Make a well in the center of the flour mixture and pour the activated beer-yeast mixture into it.
Add the olive oil and sugar (if using) to the well.
Gradually incorporate the flour into the liquid, stirring with a wooden spoon or your hands until a dough forms.
Knead the dough on a floured surface for about 10-15 minutes until it is smooth and elastic.
Place the dough in a lightly oiled bowl, cover it with a damp cloth, and let it rise in a warm place for 1-2 hours or until it doubles in size.
Preheat your oven to 200°C (400°F).
Punch down the risen dough and turn it onto a floured surface.
Shape the dough into a round or oval loaf and place it on a parchment-lined or floured baking sheet.
Allow the bread to rest for an additional 15-20 minutes.
Using a sharp knife, make a few slashes on the top of the bread.
Bake in the preheated oven for 30-35 minutes or until the crust is golden brown, and the bread sounds hollow when tapped.
Cool the Pain à la Bière on a wire rack before slicing.

Enjoy your homemade Beer Bread, which has a unique flavor and a hint of the beer used in the recipe. It's a simple and delicious bread that pairs well with a variety of dishes!

**Pain à la Châtaigne**

Ingredients:

- 300g chestnut flour
- 200g bread flour
- 10g salt
- 7g active dry yeast
- 300ml lukewarm water
- 3 tablespoons olive oil

Instructions:

In a small bowl, combine the lukewarm water and active dry yeast. Allow it to sit for 5-10 minutes until the mixture becomes frothy.
In a large mixing bowl, combine the chestnut flour, bread flour, and salt.
Make a well in the center of the flour mixture and pour the activated yeast mixture into it.
Add the olive oil to the well.
Gradually incorporate the flour into the liquid, stirring with a wooden spoon or your hands until a dough forms.
Knead the dough on a floured surface for about 10-15 minutes until it is smooth and elastic.
Place the dough in a lightly oiled bowl, cover it with a damp cloth, and let it rise in a warm place for 1-2 hours or until it doubles in size.
Preheat your oven to 200°C (400°F).
Punch down the risen dough and turn it onto a floured surface.
Shape the dough into a round or oval loaf and place it on a parchment-lined or floured baking sheet.
Allow the bread to rest for an additional 15-20 minutes.
Using a sharp knife, make a few slashes on the top of the bread.
Bake in the preheated oven for 30-35 minutes or until the crust is golden brown, and the bread sounds hollow when tapped.
Cool the Pain à la Châtaigne on a wire rack before slicing.

Enjoy your homemade Chestnut Bread, which has a unique flavor and a nutty undertone from the chestnut flour! It's a delightful choice for a rustic and hearty bread.

**Pain de Pesto**

Ingredients:

- 500g bread flour
- 10g salt
- 7g active dry yeast
- 300ml lukewarm water
- 3 tablespoons olive oil
- 1/2 cup prepared basil pesto

Instructions:

In a small bowl, combine the lukewarm water and active dry yeast. Allow it to sit for 5-10 minutes until the mixture becomes frothy.
In a large mixing bowl, combine the bread flour and salt.
Make a well in the center of the flour mixture and pour the activated yeast mixture into it.
Add the olive oil to the well.
Gradually incorporate the flour into the liquid, stirring with a wooden spoon or your hands until a dough forms.
Knead the dough on a floured surface for about 10-15 minutes until it is smooth and elastic.
Place the dough in a lightly oiled bowl, cover it with a damp cloth, and let it rise in a warm place for 1-2 hours or until it doubles in size.
Preheat your oven to 200°C (400°F).
Punch down the risen dough and turn it onto a floured surface.
Flatten the dough and spread the prepared basil pesto evenly over it.
Fold and knead the dough to distribute the pesto evenly throughout.
Shape the dough into a round or oval loaf and place it on a parchment-lined or floured baking sheet.
Allow the bread to rest for an additional 15-20 minutes.
Using a sharp knife, make a few slashes on the top of the bread.
Bake in the preheated oven for 30-35 minutes or until the crust is golden brown, and the bread sounds hollow when tapped.
Cool the Pain de Pesto on a wire rack before slicing.

Enjoy your homemade Pesto Bread with the delightful flavors of basil, garlic, and Parmesan! It's a fantastic bread to serve on its own or alongside pasta dishes.

**Pain aux Épinards**

Ingredients:

- 500g bread flour
- 10g salt
- 7g active dry yeast
- 300ml lukewarm water
- 3 tablespoons olive oil
- 1 cup fresh spinach, finely chopped
- 1/2 cup feta cheese, crumbled (optional)
- 1/4 cup pine nuts (optional)
- 1 teaspoon dried oregano
- 1 teaspoon dried basil

Instructions:

In a small bowl, combine the lukewarm water and active dry yeast. Allow it to sit for 5-10 minutes until the mixture becomes frothy.
In a large mixing bowl, combine the bread flour and salt.
Make a well in the center of the flour mixture and pour the activated yeast mixture into it.
Add the olive oil to the well.
Gradually incorporate the flour into the liquid, stirring with a wooden spoon or your hands until a dough forms.
Knead the dough on a floured surface for about 10-15 minutes until it is smooth and elastic.
Place the dough in a lightly oiled bowl, cover it with a damp cloth, and let it rise in a warm place for 1-2 hours or until it doubles in size.
Preheat your oven to 200°C (400°F).
Punch down the risen dough and turn it onto a floured surface.
Spread the finely chopped fresh spinach, crumbled feta cheese (if using), pine nuts (if using), dried oregano, and dried basil over the dough.
Fold and knead the dough to distribute the ingredients evenly throughout.
Shape the dough into a round or oval loaf and place it on a parchment-lined or floured baking sheet.
Allow the bread to rest for an additional 15-20 minutes.
Using a sharp knife, make a few slashes on the top of the bread.

Bake in the preheated oven for 30-35 minutes or until the crust is golden brown, and the bread sounds hollow when tapped.
Cool the Pain aux Épinards on a wire rack before slicing.

Enjoy your homemade Spinach Bread with the added goodness of fresh spinach! It's a flavorful and nutritious option that pairs well with various meals.

**Pain aux Champignons**

Ingredients:

- 500g bread flour
- 10g salt
- 7g active dry yeast
- 300ml lukewarm water
- 3 tablespoons olive oil
- 200g fresh mushrooms, finely chopped
- 1/2 cup grated Gruyère cheese (optional)
- 1 teaspoon dried thyme
- 1 teaspoon dried rosemary
- Salt and pepper to taste

Instructions:

In a small bowl, combine the lukewarm water and active dry yeast. Allow it to sit for 5-10 minutes until the mixture becomes frothy.
In a large mixing bowl, combine the bread flour and salt.
Make a well in the center of the flour mixture and pour the activated yeast mixture into it.
Add the olive oil to the well.
Gradually incorporate the flour into the liquid, stirring with a wooden spoon or your hands until a dough forms.
Knead the dough on a floured surface for about 10-15 minutes until it is smooth and elastic.
Place the dough in a lightly oiled bowl, cover it with a damp cloth, and let it rise in a warm place for 1-2 hours or until it doubles in size.
Preheat your oven to 200°C (400°F).
Punch down the risen dough and turn it onto a floured surface.
Spread the finely chopped mushrooms evenly over the dough.
Sprinkle dried thyme and rosemary over the mushrooms. Season with salt and pepper to taste.
Fold and knead the dough to distribute the mushrooms and herbs evenly throughout.
Shape the dough into a round or oval loaf and place it on a parchment-lined or floured baking sheet.
Optional: Sprinkle grated Gruyère cheese on top of the loaf.

Allow the bread to rest for an additional 15-20 minutes.
Using a sharp knife, make a few slashes on the top of the bread.
Bake in the preheated oven for 30-35 minutes or until the crust is golden brown, and the bread sounds hollow when tapped.
Cool the Pain aux Champignons on a wire rack before slicing.

Enjoy your homemade Mushroom Bread with the rich flavor of mushrooms and aromatic herbs! It's a delicious choice for bread lovers.

**Pain de Noël**

Ingredients:

- 500g bread flour
- 10g salt
- 7g active dry yeast
- 300ml lukewarm milk
- 3 tablespoons unsalted butter, melted
- 1/4 cup honey
- 1 teaspoon ground cinnamon
- 1/2 teaspoon ground nutmeg
- 1/2 cup mixed dried fruits (such as raisins, currants, and chopped apricots)
- 1/2 cup chopped nuts (such as walnuts or almonds)
- Zest of one orange
- Powdered sugar for dusting (optional)

Instructions:

In a small bowl, combine the lukewarm milk and active dry yeast. Allow it to sit for 5-10 minutes until the mixture becomes frothy.
In a large mixing bowl, combine the bread flour and salt.
Make a well in the center of the flour mixture and pour the activated yeast mixture into it.
Add the melted butter, honey, ground cinnamon, and ground nutmeg to the well.
Gradually incorporate the flour into the liquid, stirring with a wooden spoon or your hands until a dough forms.
Knead the dough on a floured surface for about 10-15 minutes until it is smooth and elastic.
Place the dough in a lightly oiled bowl, cover it with a damp cloth, and let it rise in a warm place for 1-2 hours or until it doubles in size.
Preheat your oven to 180°C (350°F).
Punch down the risen dough and turn it onto a floured surface.
Add the mixed dried fruits, chopped nuts, and orange zest to the dough. Knead the dough to distribute the fruits, nuts, and zest evenly.
Shape the dough into a round or oval loaf and place it on a parchment-lined or floured baking sheet.
Allow the Christmas Bread to rest for an additional 15-20 minutes.

Bake in the preheated oven for 30-35 minutes or until the crust is golden brown, and the bread sounds hollow when tapped.
Optional: Dust the cooled bread with powdered sugar for a festive touch.
Cool the Pain de Noël on a wire rack before slicing.

Enjoy your homemade Christmas Bread with the delightful flavors of cinnamon, nutmeg, dried fruits, and nuts. It's a perfect addition to your holiday celebrations!

**Pain à la Citrouille**

Ingredients:

- 1 3/4 cups all-purpose flour
- 1 teaspoon baking soda
- 1/2 teaspoon baking powder
- 1/2 teaspoon salt
- 1 teaspoon ground cinnamon
- 1/2 teaspoon ground nutmeg
- 1/4 teaspoon ground cloves
- 1/4 teaspoon ground ginger
- 1/2 cup unsalted butter, softened
- 1 cup granulated sugar
- 2 large eggs
- 1 cup canned pumpkin puree
- 1/3 cup water
- 1 teaspoon vanilla extract
- 1/2 cup chopped nuts (optional)

Instructions:

Preheat your oven to 350°F (175°C). Grease and flour a 9x5-inch loaf pan.
In a medium bowl, whisk together the flour, baking soda, baking powder, salt, cinnamon, nutmeg, cloves, and ginger. Set aside.
In a large mixing bowl, cream together the softened butter and granulated sugar until light and fluffy.
Add the eggs one at a time, beating well after each addition.
Mix in the pumpkin puree, water, and vanilla extract until well combined.
Gradually add the dry ingredients to the wet ingredients, mixing just until incorporated. Do not overmix.
If using, fold in the chopped nuts.
Pour the batter into the prepared loaf pan, spreading it evenly.
Bake in the preheated oven for 60-70 minutes or until a toothpick inserted into the center comes out clean.
Allow the Pumpkin Bread to cool in the pan for 10 minutes before transferring it to a wire rack to cool completely.
Once cooled, slice and enjoy your delicious Pain à la Citrouille!

This Pumpkin Bread is moist, flavorful, and perfect for the fall season. Feel free to add your favorite nuts or a sprinkle of powdered sugar on top for an extra touch.

**Pain de Poires et Roquefort**

Ingredients:

- 2 ripe pears, peeled, cored, and diced
- 200g Roquefort cheese, crumbled
- 500g bread flour
- 10g salt
- 7g active dry yeast
- 300ml lukewarm water
- 3 tablespoons olive oil
- 1 tablespoon honey
- Freshly ground black pepper to taste

Instructions:

In a small bowl, combine the lukewarm water and active dry yeast. Allow it to sit for 5-10 minutes until the mixture becomes frothy.
In a large mixing bowl, combine the bread flour and salt.
Make a well in the center of the flour mixture and pour the activated yeast mixture into it.
Add the olive oil and honey to the well.
Gradually incorporate the flour into the liquid, stirring with a wooden spoon or your hands until a dough forms.
Knead the dough on a floured surface for about 10-15 minutes until it is smooth and elastic.
Place the dough in a lightly oiled bowl, cover it with a damp cloth, and let it rise in a warm place for 1-2 hours or until it doubles in size.
Preheat your oven to 200°C (400°F).
Punch down the risen dough and turn it onto a floured surface.
Flatten the dough and spread the diced pears and crumbled Roquefort cheese evenly over it.
Season with freshly ground black pepper to taste.
Fold and knead the dough to distribute the pears and cheese evenly throughout.
Shape the dough into a round or oval loaf and place it on a parchment-lined or floured baking sheet.
Allow the bread to rest for an additional 15-20 minutes.
Using a sharp knife, make a few slashes on the top of the bread.

Bake in the preheated oven for 30-35 minutes or until the crust is golden brown, and the bread sounds hollow when tapped.
Cool the Pain de Poires et Roquefort on a wire rack before slicing.

Enjoy your homemade Pear and Roquefort Bread with the delightful combination of sweet pears and tangy Roquefort cheese! It's a unique and flavorful bread perfect for special occasions.

**Pain de Pommes et Cannelle**

Ingredients:

- 2 medium-sized apples, peeled, cored, and finely chopped
- 1 tablespoon lemon juice
- 500g bread flour
- 10g salt
- 7g active dry yeast
- 300ml lukewarm water
- 3 tablespoons olive oil
- 1/4 cup honey or maple syrup
- 2 teaspoons ground cinnamon
- 1/2 cup chopped walnuts or pecans (optional)

Instructions:

In a bowl, toss the finely chopped apples with lemon juice to prevent browning. Set aside.
In a small bowl, combine the lukewarm water and active dry yeast. Allow it to sit for 5-10 minutes until the mixture becomes frothy.
In a large mixing bowl, combine the bread flour and salt.
Make a well in the center of the flour mixture and pour the activated yeast mixture into it.
Add the olive oil, honey (or maple syrup), and ground cinnamon to the well.
Gradually incorporate the flour into the liquid, stirring with a wooden spoon or your hands until a dough forms.
Knead the dough on a floured surface for about 10-15 minutes until it is smooth and elastic.
Place the dough in a lightly oiled bowl, cover it with a damp cloth, and let it rise in a warm place for 1-2 hours or until it doubles in size.
Preheat your oven to 200°C (400°F).
Punch down the risen dough and turn it onto a floured surface.
Spread the chopped apples evenly over the dough. If using, sprinkle the chopped nuts over the apples.
Fold and knead the dough to distribute the apples (and nuts) evenly throughout.
Shape the dough into a round or oval loaf and place it on a parchment-lined or floured baking sheet.
Allow the bread to rest for an additional 15-20 minutes.

Using a sharp knife, make a few slashes on the top of the bread.
Bake in the preheated oven for 30-35 minutes or until the crust is golden brown, and the bread sounds hollow when tapped.
Cool the Pain de Pommes et Cannelle on a wire rack before slicing.

Enjoy your homemade Apple and Cinnamon Bread with the warm and comforting flavors of autumn! It's perfect for breakfast or as a delightful treat with a cup of tea or coffee.

**Pain de Pistache**

Ingredients:

- 500g bread flour
- 10g salt
- 7g active dry yeast
- 300ml lukewarm water
- 3 tablespoons olive oil
- 1/4 cup honey
- 1 cup shelled pistachios, chopped

Instructions:

In a small bowl, combine lukewarm water and active dry yeast. Allow it to sit for 5-10 minutes until the mixture becomes frothy.
In a large mixing bowl, combine bread flour and salt.
Make a well in the center of the flour mixture and pour the activated yeast mixture into it.
Add olive oil and honey to the well.
Gradually incorporate the flour into the liquid, stirring with a wooden spoon or your hands until a dough forms.
Knead the dough on a floured surface for about 10-15 minutes until it is smooth and elastic.
Place the dough in a lightly oiled bowl, cover it with a damp cloth, and let it rise in a warm place for 1-2 hours or until it doubles in size.
Preheat your oven to 200°C (400°F).
Punch down the risen dough and turn it onto a floured surface.
Spread the chopped pistachios evenly over the dough.
Fold and knead the dough to distribute the pistachios evenly throughout.
Shape the dough into a round or oval loaf and place it on a parchment-lined or floured baking sheet.
Allow the bread to rest for an additional 15-20 minutes.
Using a sharp knife, make a few slashes on the top of the bread.
Bake in the preheated oven for 30-35 minutes or until the crust is golden brown, and the bread sounds hollow when tapped.
Cool the Pistachio Bread on a wire rack before slicing.

Enjoy your homemade Pistachio Bread with the delightful flavor and crunch of pistachios! It's a unique and tasty bread that pairs well with various spreads or makes a flavorful addition to any meal.

**Pain de Saumon**

Ingredients:

- 500g bread flour
- 10g salt
- 7g active dry yeast
- 300ml lukewarm water
- 3 tablespoons olive oil
- 200g smoked salmon, chopped
- 1/4 cup chopped fresh dill
- 1 tablespoon lemon zest
- 1/2 cup cream cheese, softened

Instructions:

In a small bowl, combine the lukewarm water and active dry yeast. Allow it to sit for 5-10 minutes until the mixture becomes frothy.
In a large mixing bowl, combine the bread flour and salt.
Make a well in the center of the flour mixture and pour the activated yeast mixture into it.
Add the olive oil to the well.
Gradually incorporate the flour into the liquid, stirring with a wooden spoon or your hands until a dough forms.
Knead the dough on a floured surface for about 10-15 minutes until it is smooth and elastic.
Place the dough in a lightly oiled bowl, cover it with a damp cloth, and let it rise in a warm place for 1-2 hours or until it doubles in size.
Preheat your oven to 200°C (400°F).
Punch down the risen dough and turn it onto a floured surface.
Spread the chopped smoked salmon, fresh dill, and lemon zest evenly over the dough.
Fold and knead the dough to distribute the salmon, dill, and lemon zest evenly throughout.
Shape the dough into a round or oval loaf and place it on a parchment-lined or floured baking sheet.
Allow the bread to rest for an additional 15-20 minutes.
Using a sharp knife, make a few slashes on the top of the bread.

Bake in the preheated oven for 30-35 minutes or until the crust is golden brown, and the bread sounds hollow when tapped.
Cool the Pain de Saumon on a wire rack before slicing.
Once cooled, spread the softened cream cheese over the top of the bread.

Enjoy your homemade Salmon Bread with the rich flavors of smoked salmon, dill, and lemon zest! It makes for a delicious appetizer or a unique addition to a brunch spread.

**Pain de Jambon et Fromage**

Ingredients:

- 500g bread flour
- 10g salt
- 7g active dry yeast
- 300ml lukewarm water
- 3 tablespoons olive oil
- 200g cooked ham, diced
- 200g cheese (Gruyère, cheddar, or your choice), shredded
- 1/4 cup chopped fresh parsley
- 1 tablespoon Dijon mustard (optional)

Instructions:

In a small bowl, combine the lukewarm water and active dry yeast. Allow it to sit for 5-10 minutes until the mixture becomes frothy.
In a large mixing bowl, combine the bread flour and salt.
Make a well in the center of the flour mixture and pour the activated yeast mixture into it.
Add the olive oil to the well.
Gradually incorporate the flour into the liquid, stirring with a wooden spoon or your hands until a dough forms.
Knead the dough on a floured surface for about 10-15 minutes until it is smooth and elastic.
Place the dough in a lightly oiled bowl, cover it with a damp cloth, and let it rise in a warm place for 1-2 hours or until it doubles in size.
Preheat your oven to 200°C (400°F).
Punch down the risen dough and turn it onto a floured surface.
Spread the diced ham, shredded cheese, chopped parsley, and Dijon mustard (if using) evenly over the dough.
Fold and knead the dough to distribute the ham, cheese, parsley, and mustard evenly throughout.
Shape the dough into a round or oval loaf and place it on a parchment-lined or floured baking sheet.
Allow the bread to rest for an additional 15-20 minutes.
Using a sharp knife, make a few slashes on the top of the bread.

Bake in the preheated oven for 30-35 minutes or until the crust is golden brown, and the bread sounds hollow when tapped.
Cool the Pain de Jambon et Fromage on a wire rack before slicing.

Enjoy your homemade Ham and Cheese Bread with the delightful combination of savory ham, melted cheese, and fresh parsley! It's a perfect choice for sandwiches or enjoyed on its own.

**Pain à la Banane**

Ingredients:

- 3 ripe bananas, mashed
- 200g granulated sugar
- 1/2 cup (120ml) vegetable oil or melted butter
- 2 large eggs
- 1 teaspoon vanilla extract
- 250g all-purpose flour
- 1 teaspoon baking soda
- 1/2 teaspoon baking powder
- 1/2 teaspoon salt
- 1/2 teaspoon ground cinnamon (optional)
- 1/2 cup chopped nuts or chocolate chips (optional)

Instructions:

Preheat your oven to 180°C (350°F). Grease and flour a 9x5-inch loaf pan.
In a large mixing bowl, mash the ripe bananas with a fork or potato masher.
Add granulated sugar and mix well until combined.
Add vegetable oil (or melted butter), eggs, and vanilla extract to the mashed bananas. Mix until smooth.
In a separate bowl, whisk together the all-purpose flour, baking soda, baking powder, salt, and ground cinnamon (if using).
Gradually add the dry ingredients to the banana mixture, stirring just until combined. Be careful not to overmix.
If using, fold in chopped nuts or chocolate chips.
Pour the batter into the prepared loaf pan, spreading it evenly.
Bake in the preheated oven for 60-70 minutes or until a toothpick inserted into the center comes out clean or with a few moist crumbs.
Allow the Banana Bread to cool in the pan for 10 minutes, then transfer it to a wire rack to cool completely.
Once cooled, slice and enjoy your delicious Pain à la Banane!

This Banana Bread is moist, flavorful, and a classic favorite. Feel free to customize it with your choice of nuts, chocolate chips, or even a sprinkle of cinnamon on top.

**Pain de Citron**

Ingredients:

- 2 cups all-purpose flour
- 1 teaspoon baking powder
- 1/2 teaspoon baking soda
- 1/4 teaspoon salt
- 1/2 cup unsalted butter, softened
- 1 cup granulated sugar
- 2 large eggs
- 1 teaspoon vanilla extract
- Zest of 2 lemons
- 1/4 cup fresh lemon juice
- 1/2 cup buttermilk

For the Lemon Glaze:

- 1 cup powdered sugar
- 2-3 tablespoons fresh lemon juice

Instructions:

Preheat your oven to 350°F (175°C). Grease and flour a 9x5-inch loaf pan.
In a medium bowl, whisk together the flour, baking powder, baking soda, and salt. Set aside.
In a large mixing bowl, cream together the softened butter and granulated sugar until light and fluffy.
Add the eggs one at a time, beating well after each addition. Stir in the vanilla extract.
Mix in the lemon zest and fresh lemon juice until well combined.
Gradually add the dry ingredients to the wet ingredients, alternating with buttermilk, beginning and ending with the dry ingredients. Mix until just combined.
Pour the batter into the prepared loaf pan, spreading it evenly.
Bake in the preheated oven for 50-60 minutes or until a toothpick inserted into the center comes out clean or with a few moist crumbs.
While the bread is baking, prepare the lemon glaze. In a bowl, whisk together powdered sugar and fresh lemon juice until smooth.

Once the Lemon Bread is done baking, allow it to cool in the pan for 10 minutes. Then, transfer it to a wire rack.

Drizzle the lemon glaze over the cooled bread.

Allow the Pain de Citron to cool completely before slicing and serving.

Enjoy your homemade Lemon Bread with its bright and citrusy flavor. It's perfect for breakfast, brunch, or as a delightful treat with tea or coffee.

**Pain aux Cerises**

Ingredients:

- 2 cups all-purpose flour
- 1 teaspoon baking powder
- 1/2 teaspoon baking soda
- 1/4 teaspoon salt
- 1/2 cup unsalted butter, softened
- 1 cup granulated sugar
- 2 large eggs
- 1 teaspoon vanilla extract
- 1/2 cup buttermilk
- 1 1/2 cups fresh or frozen cherries, pitted and halved

For Streusel Topping:

- 1/4 cup all-purpose flour
- 2 tablespoons granulated sugar
- 2 tablespoons cold unsalted butter, diced

Instructions:

Preheat your oven to 350°F (175°C). Grease and flour a 9x5-inch loaf pan.
In a medium bowl, whisk together the flour, baking powder, baking soda, and salt. Set aside.
In a large mixing bowl, cream together the softened butter and granulated sugar until light and fluffy.
Add the eggs one at a time, beating well after each addition. Stir in the vanilla extract.
Gradually add the dry ingredients to the wet ingredients, alternating with buttermilk, beginning and ending with the dry ingredients. Mix until just combined.
Gently fold in the pitted and halved cherries.
In a small bowl, prepare the streusel topping by combining flour, sugar, and cold diced butter. Use your fingers to mix until crumbly.
Pour the batter into the prepared loaf pan, spreading it evenly.
Sprinkle the streusel topping over the batter.

Bake in the preheated oven for 60-70 minutes or until a toothpick inserted into the center comes out clean or with a few moist crumbs.

Allow the Cherry Bread to cool in the pan for 10 minutes, then transfer it to a wire rack.

Once cooled, slice and enjoy your delightful Pain aux Cerises!

This Cherry Bread is a delicious way to enjoy the sweet and tart flavors of fresh cherries.

It's perfect for breakfast, brunch, or as a tasty snack.

**Pain de Chocolat**

Ingredients:

- 3 1/2 cups all-purpose flour
- 1/4 cup cocoa powder
- 1/3 cup granulated sugar
- 1 teaspoon salt
- 1 tablespoon active dry yeast
- 1 1/4 cups warm milk (about 110°F or 43°C)
- 1/4 cup unsalted butter, melted
- 1 large egg
- 1 teaspoon vanilla extract
- 1 1/2 cups chocolate chips or chopped chocolate

Instructions:

In a small bowl, combine the warm milk and active dry yeast. Let it sit for 5-10 minutes until frothy.
In a large mixing bowl, whisk together the flour, cocoa powder, sugar, and salt.
Add the melted butter, beaten egg, and vanilla extract to the yeast mixture. Mix well.
Pour the wet ingredients into the dry ingredients and stir to form a dough.
Knead the dough on a floured surface for about 8-10 minutes until it becomes smooth and elastic.
Place the dough in a lightly oiled bowl, cover it with a damp cloth, and let it rise in a warm place for 1-2 hours or until it doubles in size.
Preheat your oven to 350°F (175°C). Grease and flour a 9x5-inch loaf pan.
Punch down the risen dough and turn it onto a floured surface.
Flatten the dough and sprinkle the chocolate chips or chopped chocolate evenly over it.
Fold and knead the dough to distribute the chocolate throughout.
Shape the dough into a loaf and place it in the prepared loaf pan.
Allow the dough to rest for an additional 15-20 minutes.
Bake in the preheated oven for 30-35 minutes or until the bread sounds hollow when tapped.
Allow the Chocolate Bread to cool in the pan for 10 minutes before transferring it to a wire rack to cool completely.
Once cooled, slice and enjoy your delicious Pain de Chocolat!

This Chocolate Bread is a delightful treat for chocolate lovers. It can be enjoyed on its own, toasted, or used to make amazing chocolate-flavored sandwiches.

**Pain de Mûres**

Ingredients:

- 2 cups all-purpose flour
- 1 teaspoon baking powder
- 1/2 teaspoon baking soda
- 1/4 teaspoon salt
- 1/2 cup unsalted butter, softened
- 1 cup granulated sugar
- 2 large eggs
- 1 teaspoon vanilla extract
- 1/2 cup buttermilk
- 1 1/2 cups fresh blackberries, washed and patted dry

For Streusel Topping:

- 1/4 cup all-purpose flour
- 2 tablespoons granulated sugar
- 2 tablespoons cold unsalted butter, diced

Instructions:

Preheat your oven to 350°F (175°C). Grease and flour a 9x5-inch loaf pan.
In a medium bowl, whisk together the flour, baking powder, baking soda, and salt. Set aside.
In a large mixing bowl, cream together the softened butter and granulated sugar until light and fluffy.
Add the eggs one at a time, beating well after each addition. Stir in the vanilla extract.
Gradually add the dry ingredients to the wet ingredients, alternating with buttermilk, beginning and ending with the dry ingredients. Mix until just combined.
Gently fold in the fresh blackberries.
In a small bowl, prepare the streusel topping by combining flour, sugar, and cold diced butter. Use your fingers to mix until crumbly.
Pour the batter into the prepared loaf pan, spreading it evenly.
Sprinkle the streusel topping over the batter.

Bake in the preheated oven for 60-70 minutes or until a toothpick inserted into the center comes out clean or with a few moist crumbs.

Allow the Blackberry Bread to cool in the pan for 10 minutes, then transfer it to a wire rack.

Once cooled, slice and enjoy your delightful Pain de Mûres!

This Blackberry Bread is a wonderful way to showcase the sweet and tart flavors of fresh blackberries. It's perfect for breakfast, brunch, or as a delicious snack.

Pain à la Lavande

Ingredients:

- 3 1/2 cups all-purpose flour
- 1 tablespoon dried culinary lavender, finely chopped
- 1 teaspoon baking powder
- 1/2 teaspoon baking soda
- 1/2 teaspoon salt
- 1/4 cup honey
- 1/4 cup granulated sugar
- 1/4 cup unsalted butter, melted
- 1 1/4 cups warm milk (about 110°F or 43°C)
- 1 tablespoon active dry yeast
- 1 large egg

Instructions:

In a small bowl, combine the warm milk and active dry yeast. Let it sit for 5-10 minutes until frothy.

In a large mixing bowl, whisk together the flour, dried lavender, baking powder, baking soda, and salt.

In a separate bowl, mix together the honey, granulated sugar, melted butter, and beaten egg.

Add the yeast mixture to the wet ingredients and stir to combine.

Gradually add the wet ingredients to the dry ingredients, mixing until a dough forms.

Knead the dough on a floured surface for about 8-10 minutes until it becomes smooth and elastic.

Place the dough in a lightly oiled bowl, cover it with a damp cloth, and let it rise in a warm place for 1-2 hours or until it doubles in size.

Preheat your oven to 350°F (175°C). Grease and flour a 9x5-inch loaf pan.

Punch down the risen dough and turn it onto a floured surface.

Shape the dough into a loaf and place it in the prepared loaf pan.

Allow the dough to rest for an additional 15-20 minutes.

Bake in the preheated oven for 30-35 minutes or until the bread sounds hollow when tapped.

Allow the Lavender Bread to cool in the pan for 10 minutes before transferring it to a wire rack to cool completely.

Once cooled, slice and enjoy your fragrant Pain à la Lavande!

This Lavender Bread offers a unique and delightful flavor profile with the subtle and aromatic essence of lavender. It's perfect for tea time or as a special treat.

**Pain de Figue et Chèvre**

Ingredients:

- 3 1/2 cups all-purpose flour
- 1 teaspoon salt
- 1 tablespoon sugar
- 1 tablespoon active dry yeast
- 1 1/4 cups warm water (about 110°F or 43°C)
- 3 tablespoons olive oil
- 1/2 cup dried figs, chopped
- 1/2 cup goat cheese, crumbled
- 1 tablespoon honey (for drizzling)

Instructions:

In a small bowl, combine warm water and sugar. Stir to dissolve the sugar and then sprinkle the active dry yeast over the water. Let it sit for 5-10 minutes until frothy.
In a large mixing bowl, combine the flour and salt.
Make a well in the center of the flour mixture and pour in the activated yeast mixture and olive oil.
Gradually incorporate the flour into the wet ingredients, stirring with a wooden spoon or your hands until a dough forms.
Knead the dough on a floured surface for about 8-10 minutes until it becomes smooth and elastic.
Place the dough in a lightly oiled bowl, cover it with a damp cloth, and let it rise in a warm place for 1-2 hours or until it doubles in size.
Preheat your oven to 375°F (190°C). Grease and flour a baking sheet or line it with parchment paper.
Punch down the risen dough and turn it onto a floured surface.
Flatten the dough and evenly spread the chopped dried figs and crumbled goat cheese over it.
Fold and knead the dough to distribute the figs and goat cheese evenly throughout.
Shape the dough into a round or oval loaf and place it on the prepared baking sheet.
Allow the bread to rest for an additional 15-20 minutes.
Using a sharp knife, make a few slashes on the top of the bread.

Bake in the preheated oven for 25-30 minutes or until the crust is golden brown and the bread sounds hollow when tapped.
Once out of the oven, drizzle honey over the top of the warm bread.
Allow the Fig and Goat Cheese Bread to cool on a wire rack before slicing.

Enjoy your homemade Fig and Goat Cheese Bread with its delightful combination of sweet figs and tangy goat cheese! It's a fantastic choice for a unique and flavorful bread.

**Pain de Roquefort et Noix**

Ingredients:

- 3 1/2 cups all-purpose flour
- 1 teaspoon salt
- 1 tablespoon sugar
- 1 tablespoon active dry yeast
- 1 1/4 cups warm water (about 110°F or 43°C)
- 3 tablespoons olive oil
- 1/2 cup crumbled Roquefort cheese
- 1/2 cup chopped walnuts
- Freshly ground black pepper to taste

Instructions:

In a small bowl, combine warm water and sugar. Stir to dissolve the sugar and then sprinkle the active dry yeast over the water. Let it sit for 5-10 minutes until frothy.
In a large mixing bowl, combine the flour and salt.
Make a well in the center of the flour mixture and pour in the activated yeast mixture and olive oil.
Gradually incorporate the flour into the wet ingredients, stirring with a wooden spoon or your hands until a dough forms.
Knead the dough on a floured surface for about 8-10 minutes until it becomes smooth and elastic.
Place the dough in a lightly oiled bowl, cover it with a damp cloth, and let it rise in a warm place for 1-2 hours or until it doubles in size.
Preheat your oven to 375°F (190°C). Grease and flour a baking sheet or line it with parchment paper.
Punch down the risen dough and turn it onto a floured surface.
Flatten the dough and evenly spread the crumbled Roquefort cheese and chopped walnuts over it.
Season with freshly ground black pepper to taste.
Fold and knead the dough to distribute the Roquefort and walnuts evenly throughout.
Shape the dough into a round or oval loaf and place it on the prepared baking sheet.
Allow the bread to rest for an additional 15-20 minutes.

Using a sharp knife, make a few slashes on the top of the bread.
Bake in the preheated oven for 25-30 minutes or until the crust is golden brown and the bread sounds hollow when tapped.
Allow the Roquefort and Walnut Bread to cool on a wire rack before slicing.

Enjoy your homemade Roquefort and Walnut Bread with its rich flavor from the blue cheese and the crunchy texture of walnuts! It's a delicious and savory bread that pairs well with various dishes.

**Pain de Feta et Épinards**

Ingredients:

- 3 1/2 cups all-purpose flour
- 1 teaspoon salt
- 1 tablespoon sugar
- 1 tablespoon active dry yeast
- 1 1/4 cups warm water (about 110°F or 43°C)
- 3 tablespoons olive oil
- 1 cup crumbled feta cheese
- 1 cup fresh spinach, chopped
- 1 tablespoon dried oregano
- 1 teaspoon garlic powder

Instructions:

In a small bowl, combine warm water and sugar. Stir to dissolve the sugar and then sprinkle the active dry yeast over the water. Let it sit for 5-10 minutes until frothy.
In a large mixing bowl, combine the flour and salt.
Make a well in the center of the flour mixture and pour in the activated yeast mixture and olive oil.
Gradually incorporate the flour into the wet ingredients, stirring with a wooden spoon or your hands until a dough forms.
Knead the dough on a floured surface for about 8-10 minutes until it becomes smooth and elastic.
Place the dough in a lightly oiled bowl, cover it with a damp cloth, and let it rise in a warm place for 1-2 hours or until it doubles in size.
Preheat your oven to 375°F (190°C). Grease and flour a baking sheet or line it with parchment paper.
Punch down the risen dough and turn it onto a floured surface.
Flatten the dough and evenly spread the crumbled feta cheese, chopped fresh spinach, dried oregano, and garlic powder over it.
Fold and knead the dough to distribute the feta cheese, spinach, oregano, and garlic powder evenly throughout.
Shape the dough into a round or oval loaf and place it on the prepared baking sheet.
Allow the bread to rest for an additional 15-20 minutes.

Using a sharp knife, make a few slashes on the top of the bread.
Bake in the preheated oven for 25-30 minutes or until the crust is golden brown and the bread sounds hollow when tapped.
Allow the Feta and Spinach Bread to cool on a wire rack before slicing.

Enjoy your homemade Feta and Spinach Bread with its delicious combination of salty feta and the earthy flavor of spinach! It's a flavorful choice for a savory bread.

**Pain à l'Oignon et au Thym**

Ingredients:

- 3 1/2 cups all-purpose flour
- 1 teaspoon salt
- 1 tablespoon sugar
- 1 tablespoon active dry yeast
- 1 1/4 cups warm water (about 110°F or 43°C)
- 3 tablespoons olive oil
- 1 cup finely chopped onions
- 2 tablespoons fresh thyme leaves
- 1 teaspoon garlic powder
- 1/2 teaspoon black pepper (optional)

Instructions:

In a small bowl, combine warm water and sugar. Stir to dissolve the sugar and then sprinkle the active dry yeast over the water. Let it sit for 5-10 minutes until frothy.
In a large mixing bowl, combine the flour and salt.
Make a well in the center of the flour mixture and pour in the activated yeast mixture and olive oil.
Gradually incorporate the flour into the wet ingredients, stirring with a wooden spoon or your hands until a dough forms.
Knead the dough on a floured surface for about 8-10 minutes until it becomes smooth and elastic.
Place the dough in a lightly oiled bowl, cover it with a damp cloth, and let it rise in a warm place for 1-2 hours or until it doubles in size.
Preheat your oven to 375°F (190°C). Grease and flour a baking sheet or line it with parchment paper.
In a skillet, sauté the finely chopped onions in a bit of olive oil until they are soft and translucent. Allow them to cool.
Punch down the risen dough and turn it onto a floured surface.
Flatten the dough and evenly spread the sautéed onions, fresh thyme leaves, garlic powder, and black pepper (if using) over it.
Fold and knead the dough to distribute the onions, thyme, garlic powder, and black pepper evenly throughout.

Shape the dough into a round or oval loaf and place it on the prepared baking sheet.
Allow the bread to rest for an additional 15-20 minutes.
Using a sharp knife, make a few slashes on the top of the bread.
Bake in the preheated oven for 25-30 minutes or until the crust is golden brown and the bread sounds hollow when tapped.
Allow the Onion and Thyme Bread to cool on a wire rack before slicing.

Enjoy your homemade Onion and Thyme Bread with its savory and aromatic flavors! It's a wonderful choice for pairing with soups, salads, or enjoying on its own.

www.ingramcontent.com/pod-product-compliance
Lightning Source LLC
LaVergne TN
LVHW061946070526
838199LV00060B/4001